# TEMPTATIONS

## SOMBRATA MUKHERJEE

ISBN 979-888569761-3

*To my Sir Biswajit Das*
*my loving Mother*
*my close friends*

# Contents

# Contents

# Preface

*From a very early age, even before I found the joy in reading - I wanted to become a writer.*

*That is true. I used to listen to the epic tales of Ramayana, Mahabharata while cradling in the laps of my Late grandmother Mrs. Gouri Mukherjee. She often used to discuss topics with me which I loved the most. At a later stage she also informed me about reading Bengali iconic stories of 'Feluda' (A sleuth of Holmesian Tradition), Professor Shanku - both penned by master story teller Satyajit Ray, Kakababu (penned by 'Sunil Gangopadhay'), comics such as 'Nonte Phonte', 'Batul the Great', 'Haada Bhoda' (penned by 'Narayan Debnath'), and countless others. Literary discussions with her was something which was worth the discussion, she was undoubtedly a store house of countless facts. I never had enough of her until when I lost her in my fourteen.*

*These were the stories which made me wonder about it's writers. How skillful were they to compose such writings! I too though of writing pieces and that's when my interest grew even before I actually read a book properly. Later in my time my mother taught me how to write letters as a matter of school works, she is still, in my eyes on of the most simplest writer. She taught me how to form phrases, how to place sentences, taught me how to use words and many more - although most of them were in Bengali. How ever my mother is film critic too, a quality which I miss inside.*

*I'm an introvert by heart and thus love to propagate my tales through my writings. I'm still greatly inspired by the legendary writers like William Shakespeare, John Keats, Rabindranath Tagore, Jane Austen, and one of my personal favorite - Ruskin Bond, whom I consider none less than a legend.*

*There are my invisible teachers who as if speak in my Heart to pour the Love obtained from Literature.*

*The human mind was something that initially strangled with my thoughts. I loved, and still love to think what others think and these made me a good observer of Human nature - a basic element in writing. Meanwhile, the topic of 'Love' provoked my spirit to a large extent. Starting from there, I used to write various short stories, poems, articles and used to supply them to my nearest friends, relatives and juniors, until one day few of them suggested me to publish my writings on a platform from where everyone would read them and know what I possess inside. And that's how my journey as a writer started...*

# Acknowledgements

*This was one of my first experience as a published author. I'm grateful to my publishers and team for supporting me with my book. There were so many influencers of this writing that I would barely point them out one by one. To list the most important ones were Nature and Literature. The blended taste of these two are something which can't be expressed by words.*

*Until then I've just felt that but never ever thought of composing. I heartily thank my English teacher Biswajit Das under whose guidance I found the 'Love in Literature'. He taught me with whatever energetic skills he did possess - a personality scare enough to be found in today's world. My Bengali teacher Mrs. Mitra Chowdhury (teaching me when I was just four till I passed my Higher Secondary) did a major contribution in boosting up my writing spirit. My Late Grandmother Mrs. Gouri Mukherjee taught me how to read while I was just three. I used to listen to the epic tales of Ramayana, Mahabharata while cradling in her laps. She often used to discuss topics with me which I loved the most.*

*I cannot deny the help of my cat 'Felu' (named from Satyajit Ray's famous detective 'Feluda') who accompanied me while I worked, and of course my loving mother Soma Mukherjee, whom I held the Supreme. She supported me in my every efforts I did to become an aspiring writer, even when many were reluctant at my opinions. Without her, in short - I'm no one.*

*I also don't possess the guts to deny the support of my friends like Sumandrila Das, Arka Basu, Pritam Goswami, Samadrit Das, Sourav Ray, Swagata Halder and others who greatly boosted my feelings to write even more and even better.*

# About The Author

*I'm Sombrata Mukherjee. I've been in love with Literature from a very early age. My late Grandmother taught me essence of reading and my loving mother Soma Mukherjee, taught me the skill of writing. I'm highly grateful to them! Meanwhile, my Sir Biswajit Das is beyond any praise. I passed out from St. Judes High School Madhyamgram in the fields of Computer Science in the year 2021. I'm currently studying in Amity University Kolkata (AUK) pursing the stream of Mass Communication and Journalism. I've earlier composed various poems, short stories alike in English and my native Bengali language. I'm also an author of the news website www.somethingbetter.in.*

*'Literature is something which you can hear, even when it doesn't speaks', I praise Literature as the highest of anything which is existent. It has no language, no religion, no grounds, no origin so is held the Supreme. Starting from Literary classics, to spine chilling film feeders, anything is way accepted. I personally however favor the 'classics' cause' it has the best description of any human character prolonged till yet.*

# I

# Eternal Love

# -:Tempting my Temptation:-

*It's been long time since I returned,*

*as till yet, my favor of tide didn't turned.*

*But now I'm returning back to my nation,*

*Carrying a reasonable explanation,*

*to meet my love –*

*thus once again,*

*Tempting my Temptation.*


*It's been six years I've left my place,*

*leaving behind my love and everything else.*

*However it wasn't my fault at all,*

*but it was the chief's call –*

*which at once paused my pleasures,*

*exploited my leisures,*

*I had to leave immediately,*

*thinking when shall I return, desperately.*

*And as for the other men aboard with me,*

*I don't know their situation,*

*as I myself is very much busy —*

*Tempting my Temptation.*

# -:Us:-

It's been six years since you visited,

But I'm glad my love for you still deeply existed.

I believe you haven't forgotten me,

I believe you're still the same,

as you always used to be.


Here across these fjords and above me is the shining moon,
which reminds me that you're not far away,

but coming soon.

I still remember our first meeting,

while we were in the King's market,

I tripped over you blindly,

but you still lifted me kindly,

and handed me a lovely deep rose,

from that very day as I recall,

we started getting more & more close.

I pray you may come soon,

so that we could enjoy –

this lovely shining moon.

Without you,

to live I cannot find a clue,

what is it taking so long?

Oh Love! Where are you?

# II

# Who was She?

*With the passage of time,*
*my memory could start to blur,*
*but I'm quite much reluctant,*
*to so easily forget her.*


*Who was she?*
*I didn't know,*
*but my love for her by then,*
*had already started to grow.*


*I first met her in the Shimla bazzars,*
*where she gave me an innocent, pleasant smile,*
*but that thing was quite enough,*
*to make my heart race a mile.*


*Beneath the pleasant skies,*
*where beautiful creatures flies,*
*I met with such a person –*

TEMPTATIONS

*Who had a pair of gorgeous & beautiful eyes.*

*Her complexion competed with that of the snow,*
*and her reddish hair was like the sunset's glow.*
*Her lips were like a pair of rose petals,*
*where beauty and royalness do settles.*


*She was wearing a pearl shaped earring,*
*suspended by a sleek silvery string.*
*I don't know why, but her appearance proved –*
*that she's a real nice human being,*
*worth remembering.*


*I've always wanted to talk to her,*
*but never got a chance,*
*maybe that's one important reason –*
*of why the Romance, still stands.*


*Who was she?*
*And what did she thought about me –*
*I still don't know,*
*but I believe we will meet again,*
*if not today – then surely tomorrow.*

# III

# The Tempest Within

*The Life is all alone in loneliness and ever so –*
*Unless someone visits in,*
*your conscience recalls what you know –*
*yet rises the Tempest within.*
*Better you live before the touch, Better away yourself from*
*this, think yourself to be as much –*
*unless you get caught in her bliss. And once you've*
*unknowingly fell –*
*there is no turning back,*
*your previous conscience would feel frail –*
*while others would be taken aback.*


*Agony will grip the mind, you'll slowly feel it –*
*although that's nothing being unkind, yet you'll try hard to*
*conceal it.*
*Then erupts your character of kind –*
*as her place would be taken by none,*

*the passionate heart and introvert mind –*
*shall be taking rebirth to one.*
*Everywhere you go –*
*you'll start to sense her,*
*life of you shall smoothly flow,*
*over each and every blur.*
*Her face, her locks, her skirt –*
*everything would feel so nice,*
*even her attire's little dirt –*
*will tempt you to see her twice.*
*Your heart will begin to melt –*
*as the feelings inside will grow,*
*a satisfaction never so felt –*
*as if hoping for the time to slow.*
*Your heart in times is sure to be hurt,*
*nothing unusual to dwell it in,*
*but everyday it's like a new start –*
*as long as flames the tempest within.*


*Let her know you –*
*try not to hesitate,*
*the compassion increases for true –*
*as it's far from being afraid.*
*The Tempt is too strong –*
*too much for you to hold,*
*although don't get me wrong –*
*try my words as you're told.*
*Don't think too much –*
*let the element keep going,*
*situations by happenstance are often such –*
*as it keeps the Tempt flowing.*

*'Love' never ends here –*
*as it's the desire of keen,*
*the world is in it's daymare –*
*as is the Tempest within.*

# IV
# I'm Poisoned

*I'm poisoned –*
*do help me out please!*
*this thing is way more toxicating –*
*than any other deathly disease.*
*It is, might be incurable,*
*as the venom within is flowing –*
*my tempt for her is raging each day,*
*without me or my heart's knowing.*


*I'm poisoned –*
*poisoned with her beauty and grace,*
*the warmth of her feminine hands –*
*is now my only desiring solace.*
*Every day I see her new,*
*with her glorious charm and lust –*
*none dares to compete my compassion,*
*being it brimmed with care and trust.*

*Keats once mentioned –*

*'for filling him a brimming bowl',*
*I too want a similar drug –*
*to renaissance up my restless soul.*
*Shakespeare too once –*
*had spoken of women's beauty,*
*a most powerful element ever present –*
*being the divine, being the deity.*

*I'm also poisoned –*
*being no different from these celestial men,*
*my heart also is too much futile –*
*to prolong this eternal strain.*
*Although nutritious from apparent,*
*deep within spreads the bane –*
*nothing is what it seems,*
*as my self had begun to wane.*

*I'm still poisoned –*
*and there seems to be no cure,*
*I'm longing for what's ahead –*
*yet still is unable to stand sure.*

# V
# Why only Heart gets hurt?:-

*Why only Heart gets hurt?*
*There may be many more places,*
*where my agony could leave its traces.*
*I can't bear the Heart's pain,*
*as its function- is one of my body's main.*

*I can't stress my Heart so much,*
*as it's the first material of my life,*
*but by now it had learnt –*
*how to face countless number of strife.*
*Why only Heart gets hurt?*
*I can't bear it anymore,*
*isn't there any other place,*
*where my inner pain could store?*

*Often times I rebuked my Heart,*
*not to carry my moans alone,*

*"You foolish thing!*
*who told you take the pain –*
*all by your own?"*

*Why only my Heart gets hurt?*
*I still cannot get –*
*but to know that I'm in a hurry,*
*so that in future, I won't regret.*

# VI

# Thy shard in my Heart

*Remove thy Shard in my Heart!*
*it doth strikes really hard,*
*my fragile body against this –*
*didst fail to turn a sturdy guard!*
*I know not when it got in,*
*I know not how long it had been,*
*but I know that it surely didst –*
*fueling up my desire of keen!*

*Remove thy shard in my Heart!*
*I can't deny it being a precise dart,*
*it doth halts me even –*
*to renaissance up a proper start!*
*Who can take this icicle out?*
*I dost still possess the dought,*
*thou! lustrous Lady, who put in –*
*is the only one I rely about!*

*Remove thy shard in my Heart!*
*I name it as thy skilled art,*
*thou also must know it well –*
*that thy 'Love' didst successfully impart!*
*Death is jealous of my lovely living,*
*as it's better among countless being,*
*this impalement also didst fail to resist –*
*something what's beyond of any ordinary's seen!*

# VII

# I don't want to see Light anymore

*I don't want to see light anymore,*
*as she betrayed me –*
*I've now met with Darkness,*
*who really do understands me.*
*Till this stage of my life,*
*I faced numerous number of strife,*
*yet no one lent a helping hand –*
*no one was there to provide any frankness,*
*even light too betrayed me, as I told earlier –*
*so I made friendship with Darkness.*


*I don't want to see Light anymore,*
*she turned me out so soon –*
*but as for Darkness, she is far better,*
*she allows me to see the full night's moon.*
*I walk through the cobbled streets all alone,*
*occasionally looking at my memory watch –*

*only to see how much time had flown.*
*Darkness walks with me too,*
*but I can't see her due to her hue –*
*which is quite similar to the midnight's view.*


*I don't want to see Light anymore,*
*as she displayed the people's grudge against me.*
*I could see their real faces for her –*
*but I still thank to Darkness,*
*who made those heartbreaking memories blur.*
*I really don't want to see Light anymore,*
*as she left me all alone in loneliness,*
*but I want to thank my new friend Darkness,*
*as without relying on any situation –*
*she accepted me with her utmost kindness.*

# VIII

# The Mistress of my dreams

*Thy didst took my sleep,*
*thou dost swim in my turbulent streams,*
*thee is the lady whom I keep –*
*coroneted as the 'Mistress of my dreams!'*
*I see thou every elsewhere,*
*anywhere my self doth go –*
*that lewd lust of thine in air,*
*is what the mass failed to know.*


*Thou visit me each night,*
*yet still I praise thou even in day,*
*the darkest of room which thee light –*
*doth feeds my unusual dismay!*
*Thou refrain me from being awake,*
*or not dost let me sleep,*
*enchantment is what thee make –*
*drowning my heart, down in deep.*

*I see the portrait of thine,*
*like Bassanio said, 'That demi-god artistic creation!'*
*thee already theft the heart of mine,*
*yet I didst failed to know the celestial relation.*
*My sight lost it's unbiased vision,*
*as thine seat is now placed supreme –*
*my self is reluctant to accept any treason,*
*as no thing's made of no such being!*


*From thy sanctorum temple,*
*falls down those crimson locks,*
*I'm amazed at this assets of ample,*
*as in the littlest of body, how it doth stocks!*
*Then thou carry thine fairest of skin,*
*a translucent among all thy feauture,*
*so much beauty till thou hadst carried been –*
*a quality rare, among the rarest of creature!*


*In mortal, I can't recall thee –*
*my eyes, my mind fails in too,*
*even after the hardest remembrance of mine,*
*I failed to find the thine in thou.*
*The beauty thou dost keep,*
*with the adornment of thy attire –*
*a charming thing which one may seek,*
*the longing of my Heart's desire!*


*I try to forge thou out –*
*yet meanwhile reluctant at the same,*

TEMPTATIONS

*my self trial is still at dought,*
*as I know not, even thy name.*
*There's countless of why I'm fond of thee,*
*thou is statelier than a thousand Queens,*
*nothing of thee is delusive of me,*
*forget not, thou art the Mistress of my dreams!*


*Who are thee?*
*thou never dost tell –*
*only thine grace is what I see,*
*whilst on my turbulent mind, thee smoothly dost sail!*
*I kneel for thy voice,*
*I pray thee to let me pleasure it,*
*although it's thy sole choice –*
*but the minimalist of all won't hurt a bit!*


*Dost return me my sleep!*
*or please dost show thy self in all,*
*my present desire which I only keep –*
*is to learn thy divine eternal call!*
*Dost return me my heart,*
*or better dost keep it with thee,*
*inside it, there already lies thine part –*
*as there's scarcely anything left of me!*
*Thou takest my everything,*
*which even includes my daring heart!*
*presently show me how to survive a thing –*
*as my soul's also under thy dart!*

*Dost let me know thou all,*
*the fairest of everything which seems,*
*take me to thy grandest of hall –*
*the Loving Mistress of all my dreams!*

# IX

# Be Grateful

*Be grateful as a human,*
*for you can perceive this thing,*
*this celestial joy isn't felt by,*
*each and every ordinary being.*


*Be grateful being gifted a mind,*
*which can reason out things all day,*
*be glad for possessing this power,*
*a happiness felt within the rising dismay!*


*Be grateful for such a Heart,*
*which can do 'Love' with all of it,*
*be grateful to the lady you admire –*
*as she succeeded taking inside a seat.*

# X
# Fit for me

*The mind is a strange business,*
*yet you can be the owner of the same,*
*you don't require anything else –*
*once you learn to play the game.*


*Love is a game,*
*where each side always do lose,*
*no specific reason exists for it,*
*it's a matter you yourself do choose.*


*This world has billions,*
*my pure lover would anywhere be,*
*I'm in search for her –*
*that mysterious lady, fit for me!*
*I guess she's already born,*
*maybe waiting by the sea,*
*or anywhere else she might be sitting –*
*dreaming in there, just like me.*

*I wonder how she would look like,*
*both from outside and in,*
*I'm eager to meet her once,*
*extinguishing the flame, burning within.*
*Does she know of what I think?*
*Does she know 'how Love would be?*
*Does she know that she is it? –*
*that charming girl, fit for me?*


*In this vast place,*
*how would I find her?*
*the distant image of so many faces,*
*makes the memory messy and blur.*
*But let me get a glimpse of her,*
*and I'll show the inner lit fire!*
*let the memory be lost alone,*
*as it's an infant to my heart's desire!*


*How would she sound like?*
*I think all day,*
*the mind inside gets lost within –*
*while beruffles up my inner dismay!*
*How would her eyes be like?*
*darkish brown? or turquoise blue?*
*these are fewest of her attributes,*
*which I hope, I do luckily knew.*


*Days aren't moving,*

*or maybe I'm seated still,*
*I want to sense that girl,*
*with her ecastic voice – melodious and shrill.*
*I can feel her sanctorum soul,*
*yet truly can't carve her beauty,*
*although if the inner's so pure –*
*then the outside's ought to be gaiety!*


*Fate is a structure itself,*
*scarcely designed for one to see,*
*let this power elope me with –*
*that dreamy girl, who sits within me!*

# XI

# To Jessica

*It's been long since we met,*
*hoping for it to happen again,*
*this one chance I mustn't regret –*
*let me tell you this, whilst still being sane.*
*You remember our first meeting?*
*downhill the plains, and a river flowing beside?*
*there on it's grass were you sitting –*
*competing the looks of a new born bride!*


*I did found you there,*
*looking up at the sunbathed sky,*
*my interest on you took a great care –*
*although I was just a passerby.*
*Talking to you was tough,*
*until you turned about to give a smile,*
*and that thing was quite enough –*
*to make my heart race a mile!*

*You stood forward and named you,*
*'Jessica!', oh what a celestial voice!*
*I instantly did melt for you –*
*as you left me with no other choice!*
*Your silvery braid, your turquoise eye,*
*everything is so tempting –*
*this gifted beauty can never lie,*
*as your personality too, is worth a thing!*


*Then over my writing bench,*
*the letters started to pile,*
*with every line my thirst did quench –*
*waiting for you, each and every while!*
*Literature started to flow –*
*draining out through my pen,*
*it's not possible for one to know,*
*how much joy did I gain!*
*Yet even in so many letter,*
*I did fail to express –*
*no words, be it how much better,*
*wasn't even worth the stress!*


*Oh Jessica!*
*I Love you,*
*love you with all of me,*
*everything until was turned askew –*
*as beyond you, there's nothing I see!*

# XII
# What is Love?

*What is Love?*
*What would anyone of it say?*
*A rising tumult inside, a growing unusual dismay.*
*Any two can do fall in,*
*raging up their tempest within,*
*no science can describe this law,*
*in here, one overlook's each other's flaw,*
*it's a compassion rising inside,*
*nevertheless waits for the change in tide,*
*and here we have the effects of it,*
*what can happen when one takes seat,*
*everything has it's own impact,*
*beyond every reason, beyond any fact.*

*What is Love?*
*Love's a desire felt with the Heart,*
*a full-fledged beauty it always do impart,*
*the creation of glory, a thing of virtue,*
*often is false, yet stands true.*

*The longness within to meet the one,*
*overseeing others, melting for none.*
*you feel the warmth and grow the care,*
*a personality on which you can day all stare,*
*you will never know how long it's been,*
*flames up the heat, the desire within!*


*What is Love?*
*Even after all these, it's tough to tell,*
*it's like a stormy sea, on which you furiously sail,*
*it's a creation, a piece of art,*
*a majestic feeling – reluctant to part.*
*Andrew Marvell once, wrote 'The Definition of Love',*
*stating it the highest, all up above.*
*Writes of it the ones who did fell in,*
*a precious find, nowhere until present been,*
*Love's a writer herself, often making story,*
*a piece within read, mystifying it's significant glory,*
*Love's a major peace, often worth the boast,*
*living as a human being, you ought to know the most.*

# XIII

# Let the Winds speak for me

*Let the Winds speak for me,*
*let them know where my Heart would be,*
*let them do the day all stare,*
*let them help me find my pair.*
*The Winds are the only one,*
*who manages to travel the world like none,*
*it's easy for them to find –*
*a faithful lover, heartily kind.*


*I sense yet can't reach her,*
*Oh Winds!*
*Please help me out through this mist & blur,*
*please help me find that loving,*
*the one, for whom my Heart is day all starving!*
*Her love must be like food to fire,*
*with each feed –*
*must burn up the desire!*

*The Winds also must fail to down the flame,*
*else, I must die a death as same.*

*Oh Winds!*
*I pray you, please speak for me,*
*allow my love for me to see,*
*but still I request you,*
*just do speak & take adieu,*
*never tell of my love for her,*
*she herself must speak –*
*be the distance away and far!*

*Over all elements – I did kneel before you,*
*although fire, water & earth asked me too,*
*I believe you're the fastest of all,*
*and the immediate one to respond my call,*
*I would learn from you at the earliest,*
*when the love's intact – at it's very best!*
*Inside grows my agony,*
*longing for a voice –*
*which is sweeter than honey.*

*Oh Winds!*
*Please don't keep waiting me long,*
*as in such lovely cases –*
*my patience fails to be that strong.*
*Even though,*
*I feel you wouldn't take long,*
*inform me about her –*
*while I do compose a new song,*
*without the knowing I'm of her fond,*
*as there exists no vision in me beyond!*
*Please do inform her not to hesitate,*

*do inform me too –*
*if you see a mistake.*
*I thank you, Winds!*
*I'm glad you did agree,*
*making my mind roam tumult free,*
*please let me know how would I repay you,*
*please in future –*
*do give me a chance to serve you too!*


*Oh dear Winds,*
*do make Mercury jealous,*
*do pridefully show –*
*what speed is in being ferocious!*
*Make the son of Venus think,*
*while you do give him a witty wink!*
*I pray go Winds,*
*whilst I stay asunder,*
*roam about, do make my Love wonder,*
*be like the early bird who catches the worm,*
*while pay attention to nothing –*
*be it rain, or a storm!*


*Let the Winds speak for me,*
*let them find a place,*
*an existing picturesque solace,*
*somewhere –*
*where we would be,*
*be it anywhere,*
*under the sun or even below the tree,*
*just allow my beloved to see,*
*that how much powerful –*

*a true 'Love' would be!*

# XIV
## Let us fall in Love again

*Let us fall in Love again,*
*for this world is too short to live,*
*drive away the hatred from within,*
*and let the Heart of us in Love do believe.*
*Let's revive that ecastic joy,*
*of when we first met,*
*still yet we didn't know,*
*a journey beloved, was up ahead set!*


*Let us fall in Love again,*
*and forget the strains of strife,*
*let's do make the world a loving one,*
*filled with passionate joy and loving life.*
*Do recall how we felt,*
*let's feel that once more,*
*that tempt was from another world,*
*something which the Heart fell short to store.*

*Let us fall in Love again,*
*and come do feel this starry night,*
*let us live the life again,*
*while still being accompanied by each other's sight!*

# XV
# Love is an Art

*Love is an Art,*
*which all can't see,*
*the life within it takes part,*
*learns it's value – just as me.*

*Love is an Art,*
*which one can feel,*
*a force being reluctant to part,*
*a thing of charm, enjoying in conceal.*

*Love is an Art,*
*an act of Supreme,*
*the beauty it does impart,*
*is felt within in every being!*

# XVI
## Of Her

*What wonder dost this world consist,*
*can never be gauged with a single fist,*
*beauty dost feeds on and in everywhere,*
*not a single place skipped, which I didst not stare.*
*Joy is nothing but countless,*
*a place of beauty, a space of solace,*
*but here I didst narrowly mention,*
*within burning the prolonged tension.*
*For Keats he said, "A thing of beauty is a joy forever",*
*his heart being passionate, mind being clever,*
*with these he didst managed to view this sphere,*
*the bewildered beauty that's stocked in here.*


*It's of Her,*
*like the beauty in a flying bird,*
*being undescriptive through a few lines' word,*
*although it's something too easy to perceive,*
*yet believe me, it's easier to get deceive.*

TEMPTATIONS

*In every part of the day,*
*she feeds my unusual dismay,*
*my pains dost starts to stain,*
*being unaware of when it didst happen.*
*The Sun and the Moon merges to one,*
*the beauty within being visible to none,*
*with all their grace the flora dost bloom,*
*and I dost feel them, even from inside my room,*
*on my place, the door gets a knock,*
*nothing it is but the nature's melodious talk,*
*everything here feels spirited & living,*
*and there she stands, signifying a supreme being!*

*Of Her,*
*my mind gets lost,*
*forget my fortune, let it crost,*
*still yet I dost think of none,*
*that magnificent being my only one,*
*a picturesque beauty standing there,*
*a living mystic I didst ever stare.*
*I can't forget her – no, never!*
*She's a thing of beauty, a joy forever,*
*for her I accept the sleepless night,*
*and all the struggles I didst fight,*
*of her, my heart didst dare,*
*a personality whom, I day all stare!*

*Of Her,*
*she's the fairy who guides me,*
*beyond of what I didst ever see,*
*between the streams and up in the hill,*
*where everything's moving & I stand still.*

'Why art thou so beautiful I see?
Glorious is thine all visible to me.
Why thy locks dost falls through in?
Why it lustres, the beauty within?
Why thy eyes art full of dreams?
Why thou art exactly like – what it seems?
Why thou took my peace & all?
Why it's so sweet, thine eternal call?
What is it which makes though shine?
Why thou art always, present in my wine?

'Answer me all these for me to stay,
answer me before I forever do lay'.
These are nothing but only of Her,
Love's a powerful thing – reluctant to blur!

# XVII

# The Day when we started and the Night when we parted

*Oh my Love,*
*I pray thee remember our day,*
*when all of it didst start,*
*those memories of us will dost stay,*
*inside our passionate Heart.*
*The sun shone up above high,*
*while the clouds paved way standing ajar,*
*illuminated was the every bit of sky,*
*making sharp everything, nevertheless being far.*
*Dost remember the market where thee stood,*
*with thy carved flower basket in hand,*
*nothing in my life felt so good,*
*moistening up my feelings, as the sea doth to sand.*

*Then a day thee tripped over me,*
*I raised thou while thee handed me one of thy rose,*
*from that very day as I recall things to be,*
*we started getting even more close.*
*Following things went on their own,*
*and the time didst fell low,*
*the passion within hath obviously grown,*
*while a majestic feeling I didst felt so.*
*I know thou hath not forgotten these,*
*a bounded story in History's treasure,*
*the calming of tempest and flowing of breeze,*
*is what I dost regard as a priceless treasure!*
*Now thee think of what else was done,*
*apart from our regular choirs and being,*
*the talking of moon and eavesdrops of the sun,*
*even was something worth the living.*
*Now came a moon, engulfing the light,*
*things paved far beyond a choice,*
*the only sound now heard within the fight,*
*was of the battle horn and ignorant voice.*
*Mere things like clash and war,*
*didst obstacle our way,*
*nothing but destruction was near &far,*
*as one could now never of peace dost say.*
*After the life of so many living,*
*the only solace was now from faith,*
*lament I dost for those fellow being,*
*as before even living, they welcomed their death.*
*The blossoms are no more there,*
*even though it's the same place we met,*
*moon's now the only light present here,*
*a faint substitute of the farewell'd sunset.*
*I dost never blame sun, nor moon,*

*about ourselves getting part,*
*within the memories in here,*
*or nowhere –*
*we'll meet soon.*
*I know thee loved me,*
*while I loved thou even more,*
*presently still there's no difference I see,*
*a story written, worth a folklore!*


*Years after –*
*I'm standing here on this same day,*
*the same place where we started,*
*now it's of the lament I do say,*
*the same night when we parted!*

# XVIII
# Serendipity

*Thou were nothing –*
*but a touch of serendipity,*
*the charmest of female in this city,*
*for whom my futile self didst everything.*
*When I first observed thee,*
*my passionate Heart turned beruffled,*
*over every stormy tide it dost sailed,*
*a mysterious pleasure I found within me!*


*I didst found the closest of all mate –*
*who dost stays within me,*
*beyond her my vision exists scarcely be,*
*whilst I held myself fortunate.*
*My serenade was a piece to thee,*
*the serene it didst successfully impart,*
*may grow forever the tempt in Heart,*
*the Love between thee & me!*

# XIX

# A poetry for my Life

*Poetry through years,*
*have depicted every kind of strife,*
*but the only one who truly bears,*
*recognizes the real fruit of Life.*


*Through my worldly window,*
*I see those barren lands battered,*
*the winter was setting in slow,*
*while the flora's corpse lay scattered.*
*I see that shriveled bark,*
*where a bird's nest do lay,*
*maybe it's of the sweet-tuned lark,*
*longing through ages for something to say.*
*Beyond that grassy field,*
*I sense the water flowing,*
*a beauty within being concealed,*
*waiting for the cold to get going.*

*Somewhere deep among all these,*
*I felt inside a warmth growing,*
*a feminine spell to melt this freeze,*
*whilst I do stay, being unaware & unknowing.*

*I sensed the warmth of her hands,*
*the nature's motherly touch,*
*a magnificent mirage visible through sands,*
*but in here, it's a reality as such.*
*She's a time within me,*
*I do think to maintain her all day,*
*beyond her, there's scarcely anything to see,*
*up heaving my natural dismay!*
*And there's those feelings,*
*a loving fire lit within!*
*a desire inside gets concealing,*
*being glad to live this living!*

*Her charm did broke the winter's dry,*
*every living is revived as would be,*
*warmth has returned to the misty sky,*
*it's an enchanting wonder! I do witness to see.*

*Spring dawned early,*
*in a mesmerizing way as it seems,*
*I myself being a part of it merely,*
*got lost in those charming dreams!*

*Life has everything –*

*the story of a book bound set,*
*inside lies the tumult from anything,*
*a chapter starting at birth, ending at death.*
*Love's in the middle, an essential chapter of it,*
*an undoubtedly good one with to start,*
*importance lies in it's everything,*
*the principle carrier being the Heart!*


*Between birth and death,*
*Love's the keeper of solace,*
*the design of beauty, thing of fate,*
*brimmed up with gait and grace!*

*Every line depicts,*
*from where a poetry belong,*
*for every poet has a story to tell,*
*be it sung –*
*or read as a tale.*

# XX

# When a flower knows her death

*When a flower knows her death,*
*there's little left of what she can do,*
*her only hope suspends on faith –*
*a strongly relatable thing,*
*something, which I feel too.*


*She fails to remember her seed,*
*from which she took the form of beauty,*
*she stands erect among her creed –*
*depicting her glorious gaiety!*


*But every beauty do fall,*
*in the mysterious laps of time,*
*one cannot resist the nature's call,*
*whilst short while is her shine.*
*She forgets her birth,*

*in throughout her journey in all,*
*till yet she had been relying on her girth,*
*but now could hear the death's call.*


*When death do visits her,*
*I can hear the flower say –*
*'Please let me stay here for little more!'*
*Death answers in a voice of harsh dismay –*
*'little being, it's reality – not a folklore,*
*now come follow my way,*
*while I lead you to your afterlife's door'.*


*When time ends and do stare,*
*you can't extend it through pray,*
*learn something from the flower in here,*
*and please do think of what I say.*
*Keeping away everything aside,*
*I do call you all in,*
*please do not hide the 'Love' inside,*
*masked with anger, jealousy, & hatred within.*

# XXI
## My Last Letter

*I'm fortunate through this letter –*
*it carries my shriveled self to you,*
*this mistood end won't stand any better –*
*unless I was compelled in to do.*
*This flow would apparently be easy –*
*if these words fail to reach,*
*you yourself better be busy –*
*and there would be no rise in breach.*

*I need to tell you before I go –*
*listen of my unfortunate strife,*
*brace yourself steady and slow –*
*as I'm on my way to afterlife.*
*Circumstances pushed me,*
*where I didn't even sanely took a part –*
*I left the things on their own to be,*
*whilst my misfortune moved to start.*

*You are the only one –*

TEMPTATIONS

*for whom my ink would speak,*
*when you are, I care for none –*
*as the tempt finds it's peak.*
*Your eyes used to cradle my waking hours,*
*switching the sands in no time –*
*your lap was my bed of flowers,*
*your beauty being my intoxicating wine.*


*Thanks to the General,*
*for he gave me this precious time –*
*his heart is, as if a mineral,*
*but surely not passionate as mine.*
*I'm speaking with you,*
*even though its only me –*
*once you may find a chance too,*
*either in the mountains, or in the sea.*


*Listen to me, be gone from this civil,*
*it's full of trickery –*
*you'll be at cause if you reveal,*
*the essence of truth to flattery.*
*Here in, the public plays the judge –*
*whereas the monarch is the court,*
*this very mass with it's grudge –*
*has taken away my heart's consort.*


*I do leave my trace –*
*even in this darkest distress,*
*think now of nothing but solace –*
*oh my dearest mistress!*

*You must never feel lonely –*
*the fairer of my fairest!*
*For me I doomed myself only –*
*cause' I dared to be the darest.*

• 53 •


*Oh my Love! Fare you well,*
*remember how we started,*
*do keep this piece as a tale –*
*as you know we can't be parted.*